5 Things Every Small Business Owner MUST Know About Employee Benefits

by

Charlie Woodward

*"Excellence
is not a skill.*

It is an attitude."

~Ralph Marston

5 Things Every Small Business Owner MUST Know About Employee Benefits

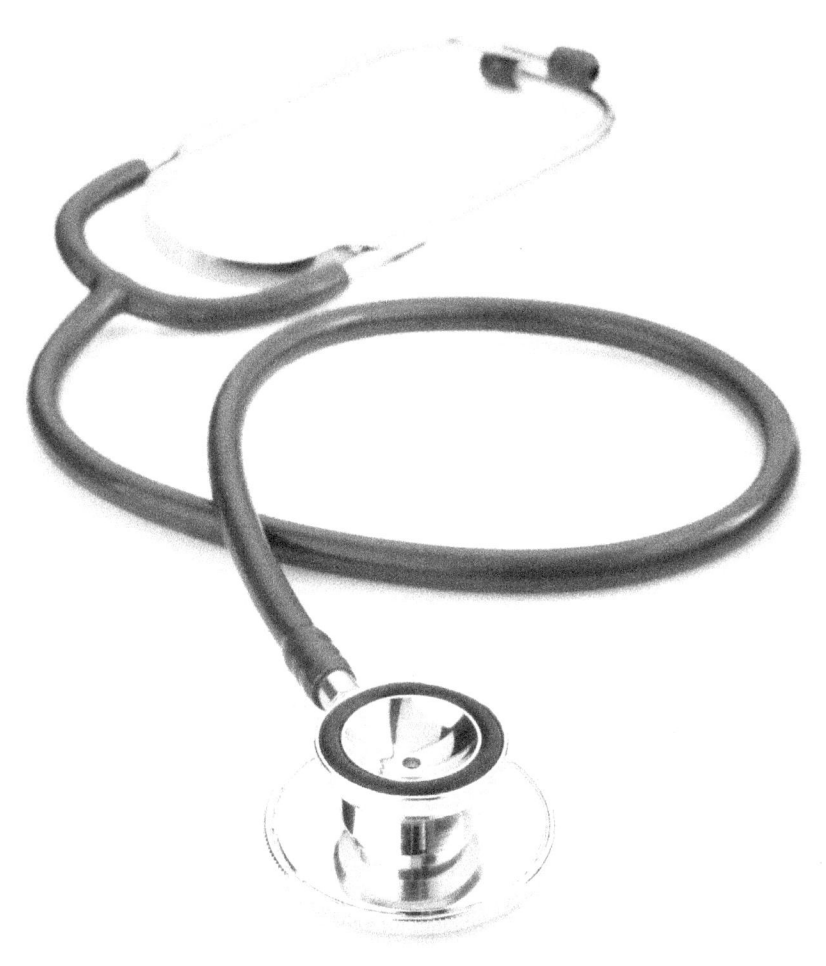

Table of Contents

"Attempt the impossible in order to improve your work."

~Brian Tracy

PREFACE

The following is a synthesis of information borne from the author's collective experiences in the insurance industry spanning over a decade. Over the years, my organization, Good Circle Insurance, has had the good fortune to meet with numerous small business owners in a myriad of disparate industries. Again, and again, we encountered similar challenges stemming from misconceptions and lack of information. We do not blame the business owners for being unversed in insurance matters. We well know the breadth of confusing, poorly-stated material accompanying its statutes and policies.

In addition, rules and laws constantly change, forcing agents to continually educate themselves to stay relevant. Because I am a small business owner too, I understand just how precious your time is and how challenging it is to learn all the complex issues associated with insurance benefits. In fact, insurance can be so complicated, it can feel at times like learning a whole new language.

Beyond that, I know your focus can be limited when growing your business. It's inconceivable to imagine you possessing the bandwidth to explore every facet of

BENEFiTS

this dense subject. Your valuable time is better spent doing what you do best, being the expert in your field, and of course, managing your company.

In the interest of time, I have carefully synthesized the following information into a short, handy guide you can complete in one sitting. It is my hope this content will demystify the most pressing concerns pertaining to employee benefits, allowing you to make the best decisions for your business.

I am of the mind that information is empowerment. By sharing my knowledge with you, I hope to enable you to better succeed in attracting and retaining employees, the lifeblood of your organization. I tried to write this book in the simplest language, employing case study examples to illustrate concepts in a down-to-earth manner. However, should there be any confusion or if you have questions, please do not hesitate to contact me. I'm here to help you.

"A person
who feels
appreciated
will always do
more than what
is expected."

~Author Unknown

Your Pain Point

First, allow me to define what I mean by small businesses. These are independently owned and operated companies with a limited number of employees. The Small Business Administration (SBA) has established certain criteria defining this designation. Typically, it's any company employing 5 to 500 workers. When it comes to retail and service, receipts may not exceed $21.5 million. Various other industries can include, but are not limited to, restaurant owners, marketing companies, property management companies, law firms, tech industries, dentists, gyms.

We often hear flowery language from our politicians celebrating small businesses as the backbone of our nation. Their soaring rhetoric is not unfounded. According to the SBA, the nearly 28 million small business in America account for over half of US sales. In addition, they provide 55% of all jobs and 66% of all net new jobs since the 1970s. Moreover, the small

business sector occupies 30-50% of all commercial space, an estimated 2034 billion square feet.

Based on these statistics, it is clear small businesses comprise a hearty and crucial component of our economy. And yet, they are underserved when it comes to insurance. Whereas corporate behemoths can afford to dedicate wide swaths of their human resources department to manage company benefits, unfortunately, small businesses like yours and mine don't have such man or woman power.

Does any of the following sound familiar:

1. You know a business (or you own a business) in which there is no human resources department. The de facto HR department is the business owner. You know a business (or you own a business) in which there is no human resources department. Instead, this function is outsourced to a third party, such as a payroll company, to administer HR. (These third-party organizations handle the needs of multiple businesses at once.)

2. You know a business (or you own a business) in which there is no human resources department. Instead, it is managed by a so-called HR administrator in the form of an office manager. This person does multiple jobs, one of which includes handling insurance administration and answering questions they are not qualified to address.

If any of the above resonates with your personal experience, it is undoubtedly because small business owners are squeezed when it comes to managing employee benefits. Unlike big corporations with the financial wherewithal to manage robust staffs, lean and mean small businesses have to figure things out on their duct-taping elements of their organization to keep their employees happy while trying to turn a profit.

Most, if not all these companies, understand the great need to offer benefits. However, there are prohibitive obstacles blocking them at every corner. Here are the major ones:

"Grass isn't greener on the other side.

It's green where you water it."

~Author Unknown

Obstacle 1: Affordability.

Small businesses owners don't believe they can afford the price to provide insurance benefits. They think it is too expensive to provide this for their employees.

Obstacle 2: Administration.

Small business owners view the prospect of providing employee benefits as a headache. Already stretched too thin, they doubt they have the requisite time to sit with their employees to fill out applications, much less handle the ungodly amount of paperwork, questions, and meetings. They wonder how they can possibly be expected to manage such obligations and still make money.

Obstacle 3: Lack of Understanding.

As mentioned above, the minutia of insurance can be maddeningly complicated, often requiring highly technical expertise. Most small business owners aren't insurance experts unless their business is actually insurance.

Consequently, they are unqualified to answer all the questions they receive from employees about their plans. It's safe to suggest members of their human resources department aren't insurance experts either. I've already mentioned small business owners and their staff are stretched when it comes to time. They don't have the hours to invest in finding the right answers; they are far too busy in the pursuit of running their business and making money.

*"Thanks
for planting
the seeds
of knowledge."*

~Author Unknown

The Reality

Benefits matter. Just consider these statistics on their importance to employees:

•   59% of employees say employee benefits are "very important" to how they feel about their job and their employer." (One Medical)

•   69% of employees report they might choose one job over another if it offered better benefits (One Medical)

•   36% of employees stay at their companies for benefits and perks (Gusto)

•   98% of all employers now offer healthcare coverage for full-time employees; 23% offer coverage for part-time employees (SHRM)

•   Generation X (15%) and Generation Y (12%) have considered changing employers to one that offers better benefits in the last 12 months (Barclays)

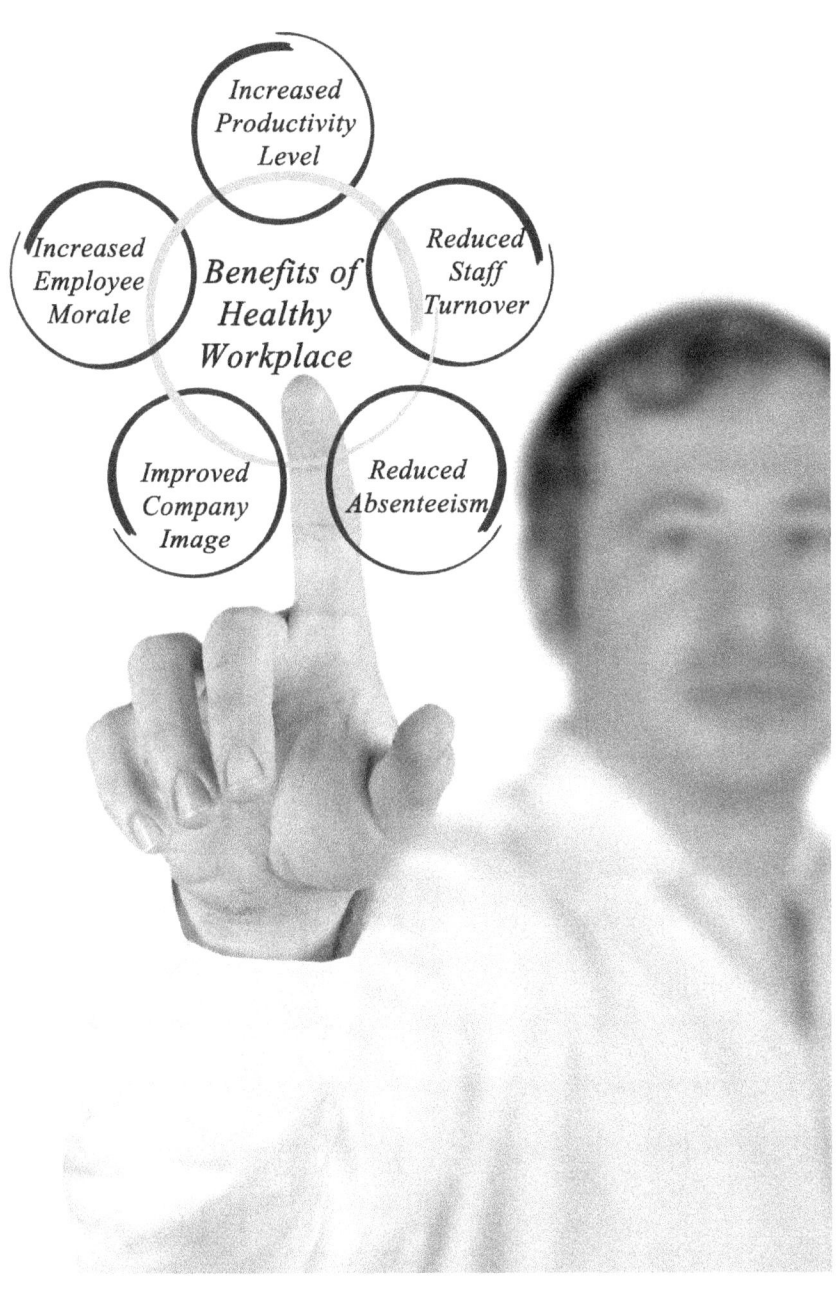

The fact is competition for good employees is getting stiffer. As the above statistics demonstrate, employees will often remain at a job offering benefits over one that does not. Additionally, the soaring costs of private insurance are forcing workers to seek out jobs offering the best benefits. I don't have to tell you, the business owner, the importance of quality personnel. A good workforce can mean the difference between a profitable company and a failure. By not offering benefits to future and/or current employees you run the risk of jeopardizing your business.

Consider the firms of Silicon Valley. They understand the merits of human capital and how to encourage talent. Beyond the competitive pay, the primary reason people accept jobs at Google, Facebook or any of the numerous tech jobs, is the amazing benefits package. Most likely you have heard stories of fun, campus-like work environments where gourmet food is served to employees along with gym memberships.

Perhaps you needn't go to such lengths to lure great personnel into your particular company. However, you can take a page from their playbook by incentivizing good workers to join you through offering robust benefits. If you initially came from the workforce and were once an employee yourself, you can easily put

"Life isn't about waiting for a storm to pass.

It's about learning to DANCE in the rain."

~Author Unknown

yourself in their shoes. Question number two (after inquiring about salary) from a prospective employee in most job interviews is typically: "What benefits do you provide?"

Similarly, many good people leave companies because they require benefits. Especially employees in their 30s-40s wishing to begin a family. If you run a company made up of skilled laborers (people making $70,000 and up a year), it's imperative to offer a quality benefits package to retain such a specialized staff. Those companies blind to this logic will not keep their workers long. The instinct for self-preservation will overshadow even the most loyal employees if they do not feel they are being rewarded for their service.

Many business owners eventually come around to this thinking when verging on the danger zone. Either employees quit, the company can no longer attract good applicants, or the existing personnel complain loud enough for the boss to listen.

But why risk going this far? You have spent so long building your company, acquiring your staff, and creating a profitable business. It's silly to jeopardize

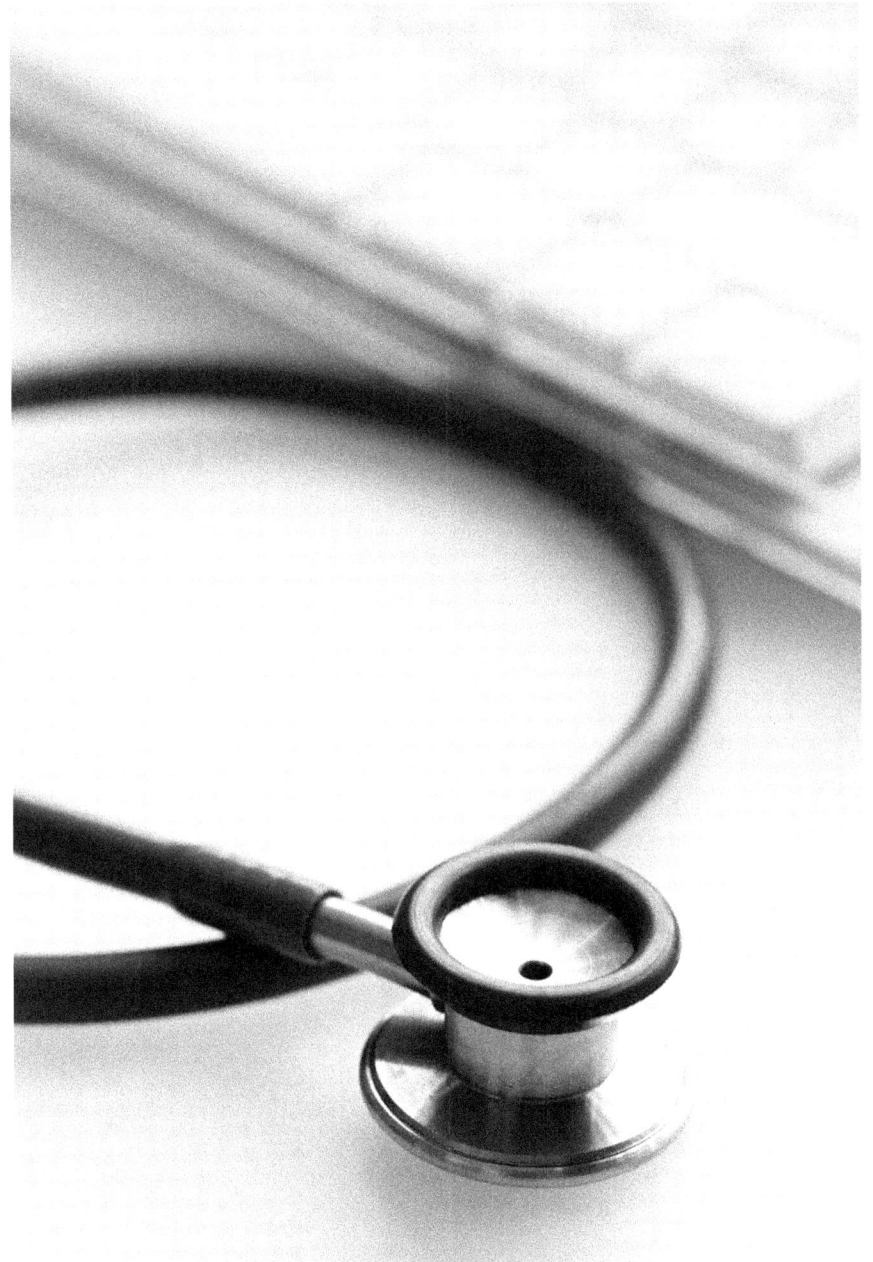

what you have worked so hard for when you can inexpensively and easily make a change to better serve your staff and you. In addition to incentivizing your current and future people, there is another good reason to offer benefits. It can help you. Yes, by offering benefits, you stand to personally receive the same remarkable coverage you provide your own employees.

*"Lazy people
are
always busy."*

~Basque Proverb

The First Thing You Need to Know:

It costs nothing to provide supplemental benefits. It's a win-win for you. Not only is it free, but you will also receive credit and enhanced prestige amongst current and future employees for offering it. Bearing this information in mind, there is no reason why every business shouldn't offer them. Just ask yourself why on earth wouldn't I offer benefits when:

1. There is no cost to my business?

2. My employees will be the ones paying for the plan?

3. My employees will receive all the value afforded by supplemental benefits at lower prices than they would ever receive on their own if not part a group?

4. I can advertise the fact I offer benefits (and still receive all the goodies covered in items 1-3 above)?

Are you ready for more good news? If you are a business owner employing skilled employees and you offer the very best coverage, it doesn't mean you have to pay more for that great policy. Here is why. Imagine there are three levels of plans increasing in quality: bronze, silver, and gold. Most employers mistakenly believe they must shell out 50% for the gold plan if they offer it. In reality, however, they are only responsible for 50% of the bronze plan. It's the law; employers are only responsible for the lowest offered plan.

Here is a quick story to drive this point home. Recently, I attended a mixer where I met Jim, a small business owner. At the time, Jim didn't offer benefits to his employees because he was afraid of the costs. Jim owns a coffee shop with fifteen workers. When I asked him why he didn't offer his staff benefits, he told me he couldn't afford the costs.

I then asked him another question: "If cost wasn't an issue, would you offer benefits?"

He replied, "Yes, of course."

After hearing that, I encouraged Jim to sit down for a meeting so I could show him how he could offer great coverage at no cost to him.

"In order to succeed, we must first BELIEVE that we can."

~Nikos Kazantzakis

He was still wary, believing this information to be too good to be true so I showed him step-by-step how he could offer supplemental benefits at no cost to his business.

Amazed and delighted, the next question out of Jim's mouth was:

"What about major medical insurance?"

Backstory: Jim very much wanted to offer major medical benefits, but he didn't think it was affordable until this meeting. The price for the Gold plan was $385 per month, way out of his budget. Again, I showed him what was possible. Referencing the above law, we explained he was only on the hook for 50% of the lowest offered plan, the bronze at $100.

Once he processed this new information, Jim happily realized the overall cost was way lower than anticipated. He was excited by the possibilities. Not only could he offer free supplemental insurance to his employees, but he could also get them the Rolls Royce of major medical insurance plans for way less than he dreamed possible.

He loved the fact he would able to honor his valued workers by providing them with such benefits. Side note: I made Jim even happier when I told him the $285 paid by his employees would be pre-taxed. This, in turn, saved him even more money on his Workers Compensation premium and payroll tax deduction. There is one more element to tale's happy ending. I spoke to Jim a few weeks after setting up his new insurance plans. He told me he was opening a second coffee shop and because he could advertise all the amazing benefits his company now offered, he received many more qualified applicants.

"Discipline is the bridge between goals and accomplishment."

~Jim Rohn

Have you been burned?

Situation 1: Lack of Follow-Through

Okay. Sounds great, you may be thinking. But I already use a broker to offer benefits to my employees, and the positive results you mentioned haven't been my experience at all.

If this is the case, does this sound like your experience?

A broker comes into your office, offering a nice lunch and learn presentation. He or she distributes applications to your employees to complete. The broker doesn't personalize explanations to each employee. It's more of a general meeting. If there is an employee concerned about specific issues, it's unlikely they are brought up amongst the group.

For instance, it's doubtful Bob from accounting will mention the fact he and his wife, Emily, are planning to have a baby and he wants to know what his out-of-

pocket costs may be. Similarly, it's unlikely a person suffering from chronic pain or illness will raise their hand to inquire about their unique coverage needs during such a public presentation.

What happens next? You, the employer, agree to the broker's plan but things don't exactly pan out. After the deli sandwiches disappear so does your broker. It's now up to you and your overworked office manager to answer esoteric benefits questions. This leads to frustration for everyone. Your employees feel frustrated by the lack of answers, and they end up making uninformed decisions on their own.

Now, you have an even bigger problem on your hands, though. Not only is your HR staff left to answer policy questions a broker or licensed individual would be better qualified to answer, you as the employer have left yourself open to a lawsuit. An HR department's true purpose is to offer personnel help, not answer complicated insurance questions. Untrained, and unqualified to do so, they are exposing you to potential legal problems.

"Life moves pretty fast.

If you don't stop and look around once in a while, you could miss it."

~Ferris Bueller's Day Off

Situation 2: Lack of Care (In Regard to Price)

Ask yourself this important question: is your current broker doing all they can to ensure you have the best plan at the best price? Even if you happen to love your broker and have no reason to doubt their expertise, it's worth investigating. Rates change drastically throughout the year based on age and location. A good broker should constantly be reviewing prices and plans.

Several months ago, I met with a Jane, a business owner who was only offering one carrier to her employees as part of their coverage. After researching, I discovered several different carriers offered better plans at cheaper rates she was not even aware of because her broker never shopped around to see what else was out there.

I quickly found her a better-priced plan. Then I learned there was an employee who wanted the benefits of a Kaiser package, but the broker hadn't even offered it due to lack of research. The broker was so lazy he didn't bother to learn about an innovative program called Cal Choice. Cal Choice allows an employer to offer multiple carriers to their employees. For instance, one employee may opt for Anthem Blue Cross, one

employee might pick Kaiser, and a third employee could select Health Net. I helped this business owner understand you need not be limited to just one health coverage plan. More options mean more savings and more individualized benefits.

I like to think I'm not lazy. In fact, I pride myself on out-of-the-box thinking and proactivity. I took the pulse of Jane's organization to see what else I could do. After learning one of Jane's employees declined to select a gold plan even though the deductible was zero, I inquired why. The employee told me he loved the plan, but it was out of his price range at $400 a month. His problem wasn't cost, though, it was a lack of information from the broker. The employee thought this great plan was unattainable due to the scant information the company received.

I sat down with the employee to show him an alternative option that would bring him the same value. If he chose the $200 a month silver plan with a $2,000 deductible, along with a supplemental plan for $40 per month, it would cover the deductible should he be hospitalized. The benefit of this unconventional strategy is he obtained a gold-type plan for $240 instead of $400 because I did my research. Due to some pragmatic maneuvering, this gentleman received

"Change your thoughts and you change your world."

~Norman Vincent Peale

the kind of benefits he would never have known were possible from the last broker. I'm not telling you this story to pat myself on the back for my ingenuity. The purpose is simply to show you what's possible with a little inventive thinking and effort.

Now that I have diagnosed your pain points, expressed the huge need for insurance benefits, and hopefully inspired you to recognize not all brokers (nor plans) are alike, let's delve into our five tips. At the outset, I stated my goal is to empower you as a small business owner to navigate the oftentimes not so friendly insurance waters. The following information is meant to further this process, deepening your knowledge about this subject while aiding your business.

Tip #1 Use a qualified agency willing to chat with each employee.

The first thing to understand is if you use a mediocre agency, your employees won't receive the level of attention or quality they deserve. You don't need me to tell you again how challenging it can be to deal with insurance complexity; I have already established the dangers associated with poor diligence and lack of follow through on the part of a lazy broker. If you are leaving the tough questions to your HR department, it's a liability risk.

Yet, so many small business owners still get this part wrong. For whatever reason, money, time, or personal relationships, they pick an inexperienced agency to handle their insurance needs. Again, this is the lazy broker that sends an application to employees, offering little to no follow up. What happens is the HR department, or you, are left to fill the information gap.

"Customers will never love a company until the employees love it first."

~Simon Sinek

This is not what you want. Invest the time in selecting a qualified agent or agency willing to go the extra mile. Utilize someone who will sit down with your employees to answer their highly personal questions. It is not too much to expect your agent to be there for a confused employee needing help. At Good Circle, for instance, our role doesn't end when we help a small business owner select their plan. We are always available to walk employees through applications, handle claims, or explain anything needing clarity.

Recently, I met with a small dentist office early in the morning before patients arrived. During our session, I spoke with a dozen employees, educating them about currently available programs. Some of the staff even stayed after the official meeting to go over personal concerns. Though I thought I spoke to everyone who needed answers, several days later, an employee named Catherine reached out to me by phone. Catherine and her husband were starting a family, and she wanted to know how her options and how to select the best plan.

I spoke with Catherine for over an hour, explaining how deductibles work and what she and her husband could expect to pay out of pocket when the child is born. Catherine's sister had just had a baby in a birthing center with the help of a doula. It was a positive

experience, and Catherine wanted to know if such items could be covered under a plan.

During this call, she also expressed her interest in selecting a silver plan for $600 a month with a $2,000 deductible. The maximum out of pocket expense was $6,500. I helped to educate her about the gold plan. Priced at $120 per month, it had a $0 deductible with maximum $4,000 out of pocket expense. Though this option was not Catherine's first choice, it turned out to be more cost effective for one reason. Based on this scenario, Catherine and her husband would pay $120 a month, equaling $1,440 annually. Without having to pay $2,000 for the deductible, their maximum out of pocket would be considerably less.

Employee concerns like Catherine's are a big part of what Good Circle does. Over the years, I have encountered many types of insurance agencies more focused on selling premiums and retaining renewals; the idea of educating employees and answering questions seemed to be a low priority. When some people consider the services of brokers, they wrongly suppose there is a consulting fee associated with brokering. This is not the case. There is no fee for our services to you or your employee. Yet, many people are under the mistaken impression they will save money by going directly to the carrier.

"You attract people by the qualities you display.

You keep them by the qualities you possess."

As brokers, we do not charge fees. There is also no carrier competition on the health side due to laws stating you can't charge for brokering. In addition, rates are locked in based on age and location and do not vary from broker to broker. The real benefit of having a broker is their advocacy and experience. It can be likened to having your own personal shopper, gifted at navigating all the challenging aspects of the insurance selection process without having to pay extra for the expertise and guidance.

Now that I have explained the dynamics of brokering, here's an important pitfall to avoid. Multiple online services promise to provide you with benefits at low-cost rates. Be wary of such outfits. Ultimately, they are just an online order taking system. You will undoubtedly discover this annoying fact if you attempt to call them. Most likely, if anyone answers, they will not be able to assist you with your questions as this company primarily exists to process applicants and secure policies. They are order takers, not accountable brokers who will advise and assist you.

What they provide can be likened to this analogy.

Imagine going to a hole-in-the-wall deli for lunch. If you asked the high school kid earning minimum wage working there to describe to you what's in the sandwich you just ordered, you are unlikely to receive an informed, descriptive answer to entice your taste buds. Instead, you will most like receive a simplistic, pat answers such as: "It's a ham and cheese."

Then again, if you go to a fine restaurant and ask your seasoned server to describe what goes into their grinder, this person may be able to describe a range of culinary intricacies. This expert may be likened to an expert insurance broker. When he delivers his explanation, it is filled with knowledge and nuance. He may begin by describing the protein and go into amazing detail. For instance, "The chicken is free range, raised in Oregon. Served open-faced on top of a bed of baby bibb lettuce, it is offset by organic heirloom tomatoes from a local farm. Baked in the oven this morning, the sourdough bread is incredibly fresh."

Now this example may portray an uncommonly knowledgeable artisanal sandwich expert, but it is still an illustrative metaphor. The experienced broker is light years away from an automated website masquerading as a viable service provider. As brokers, Good Circle's approach is quite different from these

"If you take care
of your employees
they will take care
of your customers
and your business
will take
care of itself."

~J.W. Marriott

online services and even most other agencies. It is important to us to make the concerted effort to go beyond what is expected of a typical brokerage; you should expect no less from any agent whose services you consider utilizing.

I tell you this because understanding our approach will allow you to recognize what to expect from your own broker. After our presentations, my team and I always make a point to sit down with each employee for at least ten minutes, asking them specific, detailed questions pertaining to their lifestyles. Here are some examples: *Do you take medications? Do you play sports? Are you family planning? Is there a particular doctor you wish to see? What's your biggest health concern: a large fee or high co-pays?*

Speak with your agent to learn if they are asking such detailed questions. If not, this person may not be the best fit for you. Remember the sandwich analogy. You want the verbose server intimately versed in the details of his craft, not the itinerant high schooler, toiling behind the counter until something better surfaces. Our questionnaire is included at the back of this book. If you and your employees haven't received something similar from your agent, you may want to inquire why.

Tip #2 Understand the incredible value of supplemental insurance

Have you ever wondered why are there Medicare supplemental plans? The answer is because Medicare doesn't cover 100% of costs. If Medicare offers supplements, shouldn't major medical insurance offer supplemental plans to fill in gaps? Of course, they should.

Supplemental insurance was created to fill in missing spots between traditional coverage and all the other exigencies life requires. As most of us know, huge medical costs and financial burdens can occur when faced with devastating diseases, such as cancer. Most major-medical insurance plans are simply not enough when it comes to situations requiring extensive care.

Supplemental coverage, on the other hand, can be used to cover gaps in major medical health plans, providing economic relief for out of pocket expenses not taken

"Brains, like hearts, go where they are appreciated."

~Robert S. McNamara

into account by any other plan. For instance, there are accidental plans out there that after an injury will pay for services from any licensed physician. Supplemental insurance can have other far-reaching positive effects, covering deductibles, copayments, and coinsurance. Some plans even provide cash benefits paid out over a period.

In a personally related story, my grandmother was diagnosed with cancer several years ago. My family was told there were no other options except highly expensive experimental treatment not covered by her insurance. She was on a very limited income and could not afford such medical care.

If she had such supplemental plans in place prior to her illness, she would have been able to afford the alternative options that may have prolonged her life. Unfortunately, she did not know such plans existed before she got sick. Three months after receiving her diagnosis, she succumbed to cancer. This regrettable situation inspired me to offer supplemental plans as a viable solution to more people needing coverage not offered under their traditional plan.

Tip #3 Have your agent explain to you cost-savings techniques as an employer.

Part 1: Misconceptions

Many small businesses today are feeling the economic pinch associated with the high costs of health insurance. However, this guide is meant to show you there are cost-saving techniques available for benefits packages with no direct cost to you as a small business owner. Several supplemental insurance carriers offer employee-sponsored plans to businesses of all sizes. For those of you unaware something so helpful exists, it can be a real game-changer. Let's go over how it works.

Employee-sponsored plans covering things like accidents are available for a worker to purchase at a reduced rate because the employer has offered them. If an employee were to try to buy this coverage on their own, it could cost potentially 40% more and be limited

"Price is
what you pay.

Value is
what you get."

~Warren Buffett

by restrictions, such as strict underwriting questions potentially limiting eligibility. Again, it is important to note these programs must be administered and coordinated by a licensed insurance agency to handle any of the difficult questions, so an employer's own HR staff isn't exposed to liability concerns. Employee-sponsored plans are not a major medical product offering. However, they can be used as a viable option to those employers wishing to offer some type of benefits to their employees. In addition to accident coverage, other supplemental insurance plans include hospital, critical care, dental, and vision.

There are several other misconceptions regarding employee-sponsored plans I would now like to dispel. The first misconception is employers are on the hook to pay some portion of the charges. This is the number one myth I encounter because employers haven't been properly educated on these types of programs.

Small business owners often believe they have to be responsible for some portion of the coverage. This is just not the case. Supplemental plans can be 100% employee-paid plans. To reiterate, the employee shall still receive the benefits of a plan they would otherwise be unable to get without being an employee of a company offering this coverage. Nevertheless, the

"Fun is like life insurance. The older you get, the more it costs."

~Kin Hubbard

employees are the ones responsible for paying. Bottom line: there are no hidden costs, fees, or taxes to you as the small business owner for providing.

The second major misconception is that supplemental coverage must follow the same guidelines as regular health insurance plans. Not true. Many employers mistakenly believe if they offer supplemental insurance to their employees, they are bound by the same guidelines and restrictions associated with major medical plans. Here are some typical concerns. They worry will have to offer supplemental insurance to all employees just like they would with a traditional policy. This is wrong, and I can give you an example to illustrate the truth. Not too long ago, I met with an owner wanting to provide supplemental insurance to her full-time employees but not her part-time employees. I told her she could do so because unlike major medical plans, you can specify which employees receive these benefits.

Misconception number three relates to prohibitive large participation requirements. On more than one occasion, I have spoken to small business owners reluctant to consider offering supplemental insurance because they were under the false belief their company wasn't big enough to qualify. This is not the case either.

"To the customer, you are the company."

~Shep Hyken

Most supplemental insurance carriers only require three people as a minimum participation requirement (one of which could be the owner).

The fourth misconception is that employees cannot afford supplemental insurance. On numerous occasions, I have heard employers dismiss outright the idea of offering supplemental insurance on this basis. They erroneously think their employees would not be able to afford such coverage. The fact is these plans are not that costly and may be purchased for as little as $5 a week. That's the equivalent of a cup of Starbuck's coffee.

The fifth and final misconception couldn't be further from the truth as well: employees aren't interested in supplemental coverage. Contrary to popular opinion, there is often a huge clamor for these policies once employees are educated as to their terrific benefits. Once employees learn what is offered, they see tremendous value in acquiring them and are very willing to purchase such plans. Let's relate a story to give you an example of this firsthand. When I first met with Harry, a tire shop owner in Orange County, he did what most employers usually do when questioned about offering employee-sponsored supplemental plans. He asked his staff if they were interested in obtaining

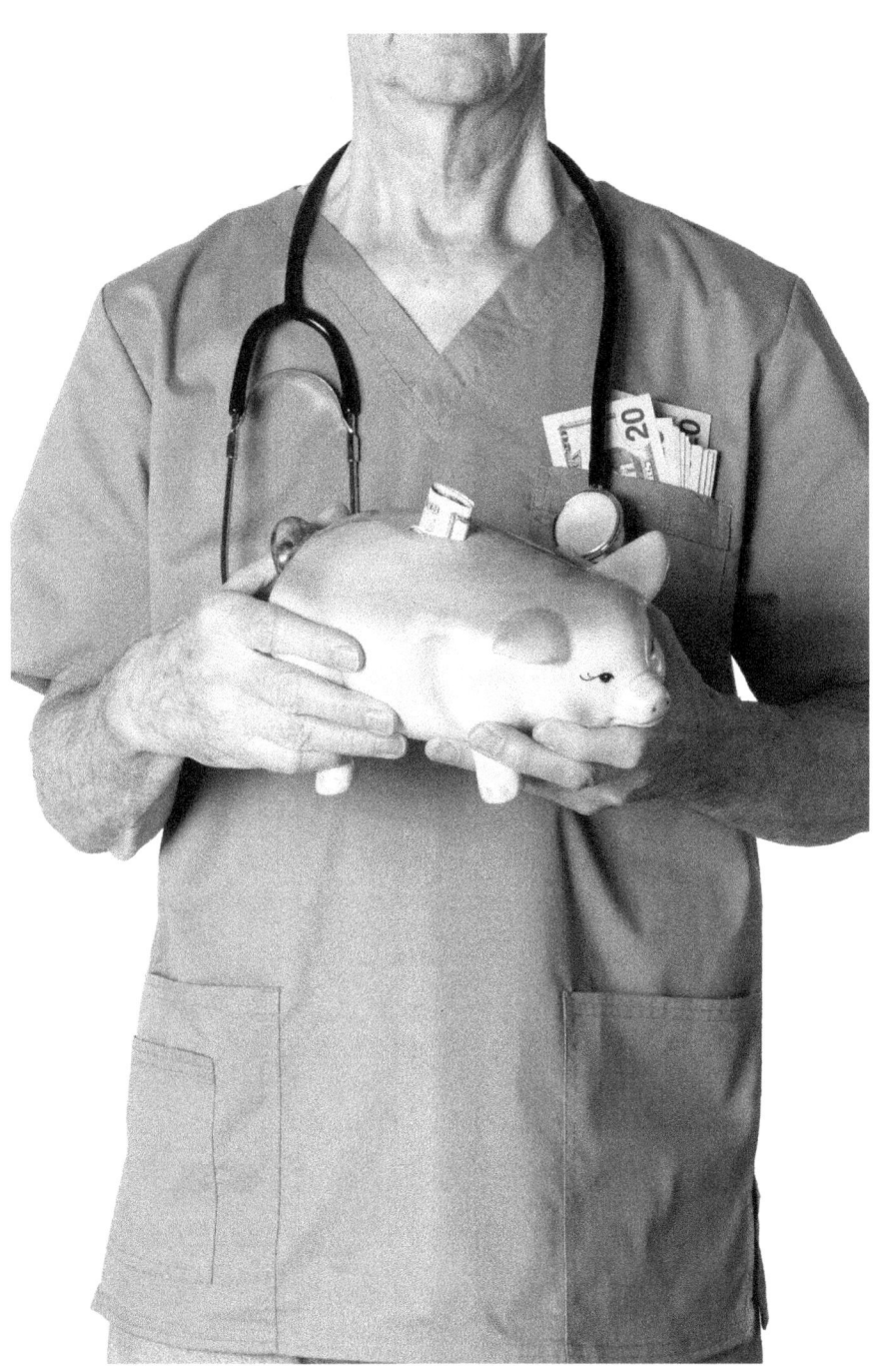

more insurance. Of course, I immediately knew the answer to that question would be 'no' because the question wasn't framed right.

I put the question back to Harry. "What would happen if I went out and asked people if they needed new tires?" Just as Harry is not an insurance expert, I am not a tire expert. If I were to ask people who might be his potential customers if they needed new tires, I would most likely receive the same negative answer. The problem with asking questions this way without providing an educational framework is context gets left out, along with important information to help others make an informed decision.

It was, of course, heartening to know after Harry let me deliver an informative fifteen-minute presentation about the benefits of supplemental coverage, all fifteen employees did sign up, including those involved in Harry's initial poll. The takeaway is most employees do want this coverage, they simply need to be informed about the ways in which it can help them by a qualified insurance expert.

"One customer well taken care of could be more valuable than $10,000 worth of advertising."

~Jim Rohn

Part 2: Pre-Tax Strategies

Now that I have hopefully dispelled some myths surrounding supplemental insurance and the benefits of providing it to your employees, I would like to go further in explaining one other major benefit to you as the employer, the pre-tax implications. First, it's important to know Payroll Tax/Workers Compensation premiums are deducted from employees' gross payroll amount. Since the monies for these plans are taken out before the tax is calculated, this, in turn, lowers the payroll tax amount and the Workers Compensation premium to the employees, thus saving them money.

Here is a story to illustrate this point. Most small business employers can expect to receive a small savings (perhaps $100-$500 monthly) when providing supplemental insurance to their workers. Though this amount is minor, it is still better than nothing. Additionally, it comes with the satisfaction of helping their workers, as well as the advantages when it comes to attracting and retaining valued personnel.

More substantial monthly savings arise, however, when it comes to employers with larger staffs. Case in point, Good Circle provided supplemental insurance plans to a locally based bank with approximately 75 employees.

Taking advantage of the payroll tax/workers compensation benefits listed above, this bank reaped whopper savings. By offering supplemental insurance, this bank has been able to consistently save over $7,500 a month for both payroll tax and workers compensation. Such phenomenal savings can really help an organization contemplating its holiday bonuses to employees.

"75% of the workforce will be millenials by 2025."

~Mark Warner

Tip #4 Don't limit yourself to one carrier. There are options.

Another common situation I often encounter involves the employer who believes it is only possible to offer one carrier to their employees. Like so many of the myths I have attempted to debunk in this guide, this thinking presumably originates from a lack of education as to the available options. Many small business owners do not know what is possible and/or are afraid to change what they currently offer.

When I first met with John, a movie production company owner in Los Angeles, he only offered UnitedHealthcare because this happened to be the carrier his previous agent suggested. When I spoke to John, he told me some of his employees preferred other carriers, such as Aetna and Kaiser, because of their doctor network. One such individual was Jennifer. She had been on a Kaiser plan since the day she was born as this was the carrier her parents used.

She had been seeing the same doctor for the last fifteen years, and she loved him. He knew her history, and they had a highly personal rapport. The last thing she wanted was to start all over again with a new physician in a different network. In addition, her current medications were all accepted by Kaiser. Switching to a new plan seriously worried her. She feared some of the medications she took would not be covered.

Jennifer wasn't alone with her concerns. In fact, most of John's employees didn't participate in the company group plan because they didn't like the offered carrier. Many of their doctors were considered out of network, so they got their coverage elsewhere. The real problem came down to the previous broker's ignorance. He had told John only one carrier was available, not knowing Cal Choice was the much better, more versatile option for his workers. Under Cal Choice, John's employees would have access to multiple carriers in one group, allowing them to select the plan featuring their preferred doctor.

It is important to know how carriers used to operate. They would often rate people differently; some carriers preferred younger patients, some older. Other carriers based their decisions on geographic location. What's unique about Cal Choice is multiple carriers and plans

"Choice is good."

can be offered together, giving you a variety of options to meet your employees' needs. Under the new plan I procured for John, his workers are happy. They get to see the doctors they like and don't feel forced into single plans that don't meet their needs. This is good for everyone involved. It makes for higher employee morale and better production.

Tip #5 Don't delay.

Many small business owners mistakenly believe they need to wait until open enrollment to make changes to their benefits. Not true. Unlike the individual market, group plans for businesses can be changed, modified, or originated at any time. The other good news is there are no waiting periods. You can submit a group application to a carrier and have a positive decision in as little as 7-10 business days. Also, because you don't have to wait, it allows you to acquire insurance very quickly.

This self-evident truth may not seem like a big deal on its face, but I advise you to please think again. I knew a business owner who believed they couldn't get an important supplemental cancer insurance policy because they had to wait until January when the new open enrollment began. In the meantime, the unthinkable happened. A key employee was diagnosed with cancer. Due to pre-existing constraints on offering coverage, a policy was denied to this individual.

"Happier people make it a point to make other people happy."

~Author Unknown

Another reason to not delay involves locking in rates. Coverage pricing can potentially increase during the time you are waiting to begin your plan. Of course, insurance companies must honor the rate they quote, but the average quote expires in 30 days. After this time period expires, it is conceivable the price could go up.

Another good example illustrating why it pays to be proactive may be found in this story. When I first met a business owner named Oscar, he was only offering Kaiser and no supplemental benefits. Oscar owns a CrossFit franchise and his employee participation in the plan was low. There were many people working at his company who didn't opt in because they didn't perceive value in the policy. In fact, only seven out of his twenty-five workers utilized the plan.

At my initial meeting with Oscar, he expressed interest in waiting for his policy to end with Kaiser to do anything because he believed he had to ride it out. After explaining he didn't have to wait until his current policy ended to get better coverage, I started a new group application for Cal Choice. Not only did this allow him to offer multiple carriers under the same company, but I also got him a supplemental benefits plan offering tremendous coverages for important items, such as accident, hospital and critical care.

It didn't take much to convince Oscar the value of not waiting. As soon as he switched over, twenty-three out of his twenty-five employees signed up. Side story: one of these covered individuals actually got hurt the week after the new plan began. Luckily, this person received a great deal of money to cover her medical bills, and it turned out okay.

If you have read this far and are still on the fence about acting because you are wary of the potential administration headaches involved in changing your plan, don't be. If you recall tip #1 in which I advised you to utilize a qualified broker to handle the more difficult aspects of insurance planning, this process can be aided by an agency managing the hard work for you. In addition, please be aware that you and your company will never be without coverage at any time during the transition.

"About 1 in 8 Americans seek medical attention for an injury each year."

~Author Unknown

Epilogue: Be open to change.

A lot of business owners don't pursue insurance for their company because they have been led to believe the many myths I have hopefully debunked in this guide. The truth is, with little effort it is possible for you to receive amazing coverage for you and your staff at affordable prices. As I have shown, benefits are a major concern for present and future employees. Offering quality insurance plans will greatly aid you in retaining and attracting quality personnel.

According to the Society for Human Resource Management (SHRM), each time an organization replaces a salaried employee, it can cost between six to nine months' worth of salary to the business. For a manager earning $40,000 a year, this can set the company back $20,000 to $30,000 on recruiting and training expenses. But that's not all. Other studies paint a bleaker picture, suggesting it can cost as much as twice their annual salary, especially when it comes to a high earner or key employee. These losses can be financially devastating for a small business.

However, beyond these hard cost predictions, what makes losing a valued worker so challenging is the difficulty gauging intangible and often untracked costs associated with turnover. Why take this risk when it comes to your business, especially when statistics consistently show implementing solid health benefits is the best way to keep and attract employees? I continue to encounter successful small business owners who are successful precisely because they are willing to educate themselves and consistently adapt to a changing market.

I am not surprised by the level of confusion regarding insurance. It's a challenging subject. What isn't hard is employing the many tips from this book and applying them to your business. You may not be in the financial position where it makes sense to offer major medical plans to your employees. However, I hope you recognize from reading this book, there are other options, such as employee-sponsored supplemental plans. Simply offering these can be a huge advantage to your employees and your reputation.

No matter your company's status or ambitions, there is a plan for you to improve your standing and grow your business even further. If you want more information, I am always happy to answer questions leading to better

"What are
you doing
for others?"

~Author Unknown

coverage for your company and better standing for your organization. Please feel free to utilize my company as a resource. Thank you for taking the time to read this book. I sincerely hope it provided you with value.

ADDITIONAL RESOURCES
Employee Health & Benefits Questionnaire

On a scale of 1-5, 1 being the least and 5 being the most:

_____ How often do you use your medical insurance
plan in a year?

_____ How often do others (to be covered) use their
medical insurance plan(s) in a year?

_____ I would prefer a PPO plan over an HMO plan.

Rank the following, from 1 to 5, in importance to you:

_____ Accident / injury coverage
_____ Major health event coverage
_____ Maternity coverage
_____ Disability coverage
_____ Dental coverage

Rank the following, from 1 to 5 in importance to you:

_____ Deductibles
_____ Co-pays
_____ Monthly premium
_____ Network of doctors
_____ Prescription costs

Write any specific insurance carriers whose plans you would prefer:

Write any specific doctors or medical groups you would like to make sure your plan covers:

Write any specific medications you would like to make sure your plan covers:

ADDITIONAL RESOURCES
Employer Health & Benefits Questionnaire

Answer each question on a scale from 1 to 5, 1 being the least and 5 being the most:

1. How would you score your current benefits package? _____

2. How well do you understand your current benefits package? _____

3. How well do you understand the costs of your current benefits package? _____

4. Do your employees view health benefits as valuable? _____

Rank the following in priority for you and your business from 1 to 5:

_____ Major medical (Kaiser, Blue Shield, etc.) plans

_____ Supplemental (Aflac, etc.) plans

_____ Disability coverage

_____ Dental / vision coverage

_____ Life insurance coverage

Rank the following in priority for you and your business from 1 to 5:

_____ Premium costs

_____ Tax Savings

_____ Monthly contribution

_____ Ease of administration

_____ Coverage

Rank the following methods for presenting benefits to employees from 1 to 5:

_____ Written material

_____ Website

_____ Slide or video presentations

_____ Employee 1-1 meetings

_____ Email

Write any specific insurance carriers whose plans you would prefer to offer:

Is there anything specific you expect of your company's health insurance agency?

About the author

Charlie Woodward has worked in multiples areas of the insurance world since beginning in 2001. Licensed in Property/Casualty, along with Life and Health, he began handling customer service and data entry. Charlie's persistent efforts turned an underperforming service department into an A+ rating. Well-versed in various elements of insurance, Charlie has worked in claims and underwriting, consistently reaching sales goals as a top performing agent.

In 2014, Charlie founded Good Circle Insurance with the aspiration of being a different type of insurance agency: one focusing on the kinds of service and cost-savings measures traditional agents neglect. In 2016, Charlie and Good Circle Insurance were named the financial services firm of the year by *CV magazine*.

Charlie is the former president of the Mission Viejo Chamber of Commerce and currently serves on the Board of Directors. He was named Volunteer of the Year in 2009 by the BIAtrade contractors council for his service to the organization. One of Charlie's main passions is helping people with cancer. Consequently, he donates to his time to the Cancer and Blood Disorders Center in Atlanta, Georgia, every year and has walked in several Relays for Life with the American Cancer Society. Charlie strongly lives by the saying: "The smartest man in the world doesn't know enough."

Notes:

Notes:

www.ingramcontent.com/pod-product-compliance
Lightning Source LLC
Chambersburg PA
CBHW070101210526
45170CB00012B/686